Felicia V. Petit-Frere

R.O.C.K.
Your Money

*How I Shifted My Mindset and Money to
Achieve Financial Success - and You Can Too*

R.O.C.K. Your Money
Copyright © Felicia V. Petit-Frere, 2018
Cover image: © Danny Media

Published by Chocolate Readings via KDP Publishing
www.chocolatereadings.com

ISBN-13: 9781793015051

Publisher's Note

Printed and bound in the United States of America. All rights reserved. No part of this book may be reproduced or transmitted in any form or by any means, electronic or mechanical, including photocopying, recording, or by any information storage and retrieval system except by a review who may quote brief passages in a review to be printed in a magazine, newspaper, or on the Web without permission in writing from Felicia V. Petit-Frere.

Although the author and publisher have made every effort to ensure the accuracy and completeness of information contained in this book, we assume no responsibility for errors, inaccuracies, omissions, or any inconsistency herein. The advice and strategies contained herein may not be suitable for your situation. You should consult with a professional where appropriate. Neither the publisher nor the author shall be liable for damages arising here from.

To my Mom, there are no words that can express the love and appreciation I feel for you. Thank you for being the example of a strong woman and for sacrificing yourself to make sure I had what I needed. Thanks for always being there for me.

Table of Contents

Introduction   **6**

Realize Your Money Potential
Chapter 1	My Financial Crash Course	12
Chapter 2	Welcome to the Real World	20
Chapter 3	The Mindset Makeover	30

Own Your Financial Destiny
Chapter 4	Activate Your Vision	40
Chapter 5	Acknowledge Your Current State	54
Chapter 6	Account for your Spending	62
Chapter 7	Assemble your Budget	66
Chapter 8	Audit & Adjust Your Plan	92

Create Your Money Story
Chapter 9	The Power of 3 Numbers	100
Chapter 10	Being Intentional	118

Know Your Worth
Chapter 11	Calculating Your Net Worth	124
Chapter 12	Creating Your Sweet Spot	132

About the Author   ***140***

Introduction

Do you often find yourself dreaming of that one thing you have always wanted to experience, you know #1 on your bucket list? Have you ever imagined what you would do if you were rich? Maybe you just want enough money to buy the house you've been following on Zillow.

If you're like most people, you think about traveling, buying homes, paying for your child's college education, saving for retirement, or buying your dream car.

For me, it was having an abundance of money to pay my bills, take care of my daughter, help my mom and travel with my family and friends to all the places in my fantasies. But sadly, those fantasies would have to wait because I was up to my forehead in debt.

I remember not wanting to answer my phone because I was too scared a bill collector was on the other end. I would sometimes disguise my voice so they wouldn't know it was me. Yep, it was that bad. I knew I had to find a way to dig myself out of the hole I had made for myself. I wanted to live the life of my dreams, which meant learning how to manage my money better. I had to learn how to become financially fit, and that's exactly what I did. Now I'm teaching others to do the same.

R.O.C.K Your Money was written for women, like me, who didn't learn how to manage money at an early age. For women who continued to make financial mistakes as they grew up, but have finally decided to change their financial situation. I am a true believer in the importance of teaching others what you have learned to ensure they don't make the same mistakes. If that means opening up and sharing my own money stories - I'm all in. I have divided *ROCK Your Money* into four sections:

Realize *Your Money Potential*

Own *Your Financial Destiny*

Create *Your New Money Story*

Know *Your Worth*

Within each section we will discuss a few of my clients' financial experiences, and some of my own financial lessons I've been forced to learn throughout my life. Yes, I will use my own experiences as examples—why not? Who better to teach you how to become financially fit than someone who has weathered a financial storm and found her way over to the other side?

ROCK Your Money is not just a book, it's a movement. We must take the initiative to learn how to manage our money and teach future generations while they're young. I also pray that every woman who reads this book will share the knowledge they gain with other women seeking financial success. Remember, money is a tool to be used to enhance your life, not burden it.

In this book, I have included a step-by-step guide that will jump start your financial journey. Each chapter provides practical information along with the necessary tools you need to create new money stories you can enjoy. While I can't promise that you'll be totally debt-free upon reading this book (after all, it is your responsibility to do the work), I can guarantee that your financial knowledge base will be increased. The money management tips I share in the chapters that follow have not only provided proven results for my clients, but have changed their lives in a significant way.

Are you ready? Don't delay — I can hear the interest on your credit cards adding up right now. Let's *ROCK Your Money*!

But first I want you to meet the younger me.

Realize Your Money Potential

"There are quite a few things I would have done differently if I had a do-over."

~Felicia Petit-Frere~

Chapter 1

My Financial Crash Course Started Early

When I was growing up, I didn't know I was poor. Really, I didn't. In my little part of the world I had everything I needed and some of my wants. But based on American standards, my family was classified as poor.

As a child, I thought the only people that really had money were the ones on TV. Sometimes we had enough money to splurge on eating out or shopping, and other times we didn't. I didn't have a lot of name-brand stuff like some other kids. I had what my mom could afford, and I was okay with that - more like I had no choice. And sometimes I would have to wait a little while to wear my clothes, because my mom had to put them on layaway. She taught me very early in life the difference between wants and needs.

My mom is a very strong woman who made huge financial sacrifices for me. A typical alpha female who never let anything keep her from reaching her goals. She had at least two jobs, sometimes three. At times she may have worked all three in one week if we needed money. I just remember her being a single mother who worked very hard to give me a good life. I'm sure she had to rob Peter to pay Paul because I was always coming home with some kind of activity fee or school trip that needed money. She never once told me no, she wanted me to experience every educational opportunity that came my way. I don't know if she had a written budget, but I imagine she was adding up the expenses in her head. Somehow, we always had what we needed, and a little more.

A 'little more', meant having enough money for a vacation on the Greyhound Bus or Amtrak Train to visit our family in Sylvania, Georgia. Other times it meant splurging on dinner from McDonald's or some other restaurant. It was the little things that counted back then. But I still couldn't wait until I was old enough to work. I wanted my own money.

Wait, shhh can you hear that? It's the cash register sound! I would hear it every time I said money. I couldn't wait until I could make my own money.

I wanted to make enough money to buy all the things my mom couldn't afford. I was around fifteen years old when I landed my first real paying job at Aunt

Sarah's Pancake House. You couldn't tell me nothing. The pay was minimal, but the tips were great! I didn't have any bills, nor did I have to give my mom any money. But of course, I had to make sure I had money for the offering tray on Sunday mornings - that was mandatory. I don't know about your parents, but if you earned money in my household and didn't save any for the Lord you were surely a sinner.

Other than that, I had total spending power and no financial plan to speak of. Some might say I was too young to know about saving, but I believe that's a perfect age. If someone had taken the time to teach me how to manage my money, I would have known not to spend my check on frivolous items.

I was living my best life in my own little world. Imagine how much money I could have saved or invested. *Man*, that makes my head hurt! I imagine my mom didn't have anyone talking to her about money when she was younger either.

Ultimately, I was a girl that just wanted to have fun, what was I saving for anyway? Have you ever had those thoughts before?

If I had taken some time to think about it, I probably would have come up with a whole list of reasons. I wish someone had explained to me the basics of money management —then I wouldn't have made up my own rules. Big mistake!

Remember, what you learn in your youth carries into your adult life.

University Life Left Me with a Big Fat Bill

Let's fast-forward a little. Balloons, cake, presents and money, yes! It's graduation day! I was a high school graduate; finally, on my way to college. This was a big deal for me. I made a commitment to myself and my mom that I was going to earn a bachelor's degree and fulfill all of my goals.

Let's see... I wanted to be rich—well, at least well-off—with no concerns about how I was going to pay my bills. Most of all, I wanted to travel the world. Wait, let's not forget the nice car and the big house where I promised myself that my (future) daughter would be raised. Mainly, I didn't want to struggle; I wanted to do more than make ends meet and live paycheck to paycheck. Seems like I had it all planned, right?

Well, that's a big fat NO!

I didn't have a plan. I had no clue how I was going to achieve any of it. All I knew was I had to get a higher education to pursue my future career. I was pretty good at numbers and I sort of understood how business worked, so business administration became my career choice - which later changed to accounting. I knew a career in accounting would help me make money, and lots of it.

As a teenager entering my first year of college at Norfolk State University (Go Spartans!), being financially fit was definitely not in my top five goals. I didn't believe that my financial habits would matter at that age. I ended up making awful decisions that later affected me in my adult life. For instance, I applied for a credit card without a means to pay the bill. Then I proceeded to max out that card and not pay the bill at all.

During the summers, I would go home and work. My first summer home from school I worked at New Rich Sneaker Store in downtown Richmond, VA. This probably wasn't the best decision I ever made, most of my check went back to the store.

I bought new sneakers to match every outfit. I was styling and profiling with my fresh sneakers. Yes, ma'am! I was fly on Friday (payday) and broke on Monday. I did manage to save money for church on Sunday, pay on my layaways, and hold on to a couple of dollars to hang out with my friends.

I didn't really care about the future. I was young and planning to live forever, so if I wasn't saving money, oh well—I had plenty of time for all that later.

Or so I thought.

In my junior year, I decided to move off campus using my student loan money to pay the rent. These decisions made sense to me then, but later on, they caused bad credit, and sky-high interest rates every time I applied for any type of credit or loan. However, I still hadn't learned my lesson yet.

I worked a telemarketing job so I could pay for my utilities and fund my partying habit. I only worked a few days a week, which resulted in overspending yet again. I had all good intentions to save for the things I needed, but when it came down to it, money would burn a hole in my pocket. I just could not hold on to it— I *had* to spend it.

There were just too many choices in front of me. Many times, it was the choice between buying books for school or buying clothes. Can you guess which one I chose?

At that point in my life, saving money for books was the furthest thing from my mind. Let me share with you how my mind worked: I see something I wanted and think, *hmm do I have enough money to purchase it?* If yes, make the purchase. If no, call Mom and ask for money, then make the purchase.

As you can see, there was nothing intentional about my process. Some of you think the same way, only because you have not truly learned the steps to building a financially fit life. And because of this, you find yourself mismanaging your money in a significant way.

The key to financial success is having a focused mindset. Our lives are molded by the way we think and what we do. My advice to you: before acting on an important decision that may change the quality of your life, consider your goals.

So, what does all this mean, you ask? First, take some time to consider how you want to live. Understand what is truly a want versus a need. Review your finances, and most importantly ask yourself, is this the financial state you want to be in?

Chapter 2

Welcome to the Real World

As I looked out over the crowd of smiling faces, I saw family and friends who were so excited for me. I can clearly remember it as though it was yesterday. The day I had been looking forward to, my college graduation. I spent the last four and a half years preparing myself for the future. You know, that future of my dreams, the one where I land the perfect job, making my dream salary and everything that comes with it. Yeah, that one... *bonk*!

I graduated with a Bachelor of Science degree in Accounting from Norfolk State University (Go Spartans!) I was *so* proud of myself. I had achieved one of my biggest goals as a young adult, and all of my family was there to support. We celebrated; I enjoyed loving hugs from my family, words of encouragement and a nice sum of monetary gifts.

This was a great day—I had enough money for my new business wardrobe. I wanted to look the part when I interviewed for my future job, which I needed to find immediately because I was graduating in debt ($20,600 worth of debt, to be precise). I had a $600 maxed-out Citibank credit card (that I was not paying) and $20,000 in student loans, but I wasn't concerned. I had just earned a Bachelor of Science Degree in Accounting, surely a corporation was looking for someone with my education.

I thought finding a job would be a breeze. But that wasn't the case. What a false sense of security I had.

The following week I was welcomed into the real world of making decisions on my own. I moved back home with my mom and started looking for the ultimate job. My mom had expectations (I would expect nothing less), and the first was paying my share of the rent.

While I thought that I was ready for the real world, I discovered that the real world was not looking for me. I couldn't find an accounting job anywhere. I finally found a part-time job at Macy's Department Store. Although it was not quite where I wanted to be, in the meantime, it was where I needed to be.

Or so I thought.

If you have ever worked at Macy's (or any department store), you know to receive the employee discounts you have to apply for their store credit card, and that's precisely what I did. That quickly turned into a bad decision, I had one maxed out credit card, a new department store credit card, and an hourly wage. Imagine how fast I accumulated a balance on my new Macy's card.

I was young and naïve, I thought to look good I had to wear the latest name brands. Of course, they cost more money than I could afford, but I had a credit card. I thought, as long as I paid the minimum on my credit cards I would be fine. That's how a *spender* thinks.

In hindsight, I can quickly identify my money personality, something we'll talk about later on in the chapter.

A couple of months later, I was hired as an accountant for a printing company, but I didn't give up my part-time job. I needed the money. By that time, I owned several department store cards that were at their max or close to it, a new car and an apartment. Not to mention, my friends and I were traveling almost every month. That's what you do when you're young and carefree, right?

My debt was steadily increasing. I couldn't pay everything on time, which caused my credit score to plummet. Every month my credit cards were accumulating late fees, and the interest was adding up.

Interest is great if it's deposited into your savings account. However, if you do not pay your credit card balance in full every month, it's added to your balance, again and again, month after month.

I'm sure I racked up way more than my fair share of interest. I couldn't pay my total credit card balance off every month. Eventually, it got to the point that I couldn't keep up with my monthly payments, rent, and a new car payment—so I moved back in with my mom. I felt like a failure. I had mismanaged my money and had to start over from scratch.

Money management is one of the top issues Americans face today. According to NerdWallet, the average household credit card debt exceeds $7,000. And for some people just thinking about their money issues gives them anxiety. They're scared, so they ignore it. Not dealing with their bills until the collection agencies start calling or they're denied a credit card.

Do you fall into this category? I did, I woke up one morning stressed because my rent, car note, utility and credit cards bills were all due and I only had $200 in my bank account. I couldn't figure out how I had gotten to that point. I mean, of all people, this shouldn't have been *my* life. I had just graduated with a Bachelor of Science degree in Accounting; admittedly, I knew how to handle my own money, yes?

Wrong!

I was in debt up to my forehead. I had bill collectors calling me, horrible credit, and I was robbing

Peter to pay Paul every single payday. I knew what it was like to work a forty-hour week with absolutely nothing to show for it. This was when the light bulb came on. I decided to start my own transformation.

I realized it wasn't something someone else was going to teach me. I had to seek understanding for myself and learn how to manage my own money. I had just graduated from a four-year university with a degree in Accounting, but I didn't know a single thing about managing money. The meaning of hindsight is 20/20 became very clear to me. I started thinking about how different my life would've been if I had learned the fundamentals of money management at an early age. I had a financial problem, and I had to make a change.

Hindsight is 20/20

Hindsight is 20/20. Nothing could be more accurate. It is much easier to look back on a situation and see what you should have done. It is not quite as noticeable when you are going through it. I have had several experiences I wanted to change later or forget altogether. I'm sure my mom would have benefitted from me knowing how to manage my money. Let's think about it: if I had learned money management skills at a younger age, maybe I would have opened a savings account instead of spending every dollar (and I mean *every* dollar). Perhaps I would have started investing and planning for the future. If I had been a little more financially savvy, I would have set up a budget for the significant things I needed, instead of asking my mom for money she couldn't afford to give.

In college, I might not have applied for a credit card without having a job, lived off my student loan, or partied my money away. Then continued that behavior after graduation and piled more bills on top of what I already had. What was I thinking?

I was not concerned about being financially fit, I was living in the moment. My life could have been very different if I had known how to *ROCK My Money* early on.

Have you thought about what you would do differently? Ever thought about what you would teach your child? According to a survey by Regions Financial Corp and Vanderbilt University, 41% of women are solely responsible for the household finances, but we don't share this valuable skill set with our children.

You may be financially fit, with all your monthly bills paid on time and minimal debt—but have you taken the time to teach your teens to follow in your footsteps? Maybe you're like many other parents whose financial state is not the greatest— do you realize your teens are learning from your bad habits? One of the best gifts you can give your child is financial education. However, you must be willing and ready to learn first.

Statistics show the earlier you are exposed to money management, the more effective you are at budgeting, saving, investing and avoiding excessive debt. You are more likely to make better financial decisions that won't negatively affect your family and your future.

Financial fitness tip: if you want to *ROCK Your Money,* you have to get rid of your old habits. You need a money mindset makeover. Badly!

"Life is truly a lesson for those who are willing to learn."

~Felicia Petit-Frere~

Chapter 3

The Money Mindset Makeover

One of my favorite quotes is: *"Whether you think you can or think you can't- you're right"* Henry Ford said a mouthful, and he was absolutely right. Whatever you think is what you will do, whether it's positive or negative. It's the same with your money mindset. If you are consistently spending money you don't have, you will always be broke. However, if your goal is to *Rock Your Money* you have to start your money mindset makeover now.

What exactly is your money mindset? It's your attitude towards your finances and the overall motivation behind your financial decisions. All of this can be pretty overwhelming. I know, it was for me, too.

But I had a strong desire to embrace my goal to create the future I wanted.

During my mindset makeover, I learned to look for opportunities, instead of seeing roadblocks. I had to recognize within myself that no matter how bad the financial situation, I could fix it. I had to ask for help instead of valuing my pride more than my goals. And last but not least, I had to stop trying to run a race and realize that my progress would come one step at a time.

I would love to tell you that I have mastered my money mindset, but that would be a lie. I still have moments where I struggle between buying something I really don't need and putting money towards one of my many goals. You will have those moments, too. I can only hope that you will think about the things that you have learned in this book and make the best decision for yourself. Only you can change your mindset, and only you can achieve your goals.

Money Personalities

In life, there are many choices and paths that we can take. Some of our decisions are smart and well thought-out, while others may be spur of the moment. Often, our relationship with money is impulsive; we decide we have a need, and we go out and satisfy that need by spending money. According to Business Insider, 33% of debt is revolving credit (credit cards), and 67% is loans. As a matter of fact, 1 in 50 households carries more than $20,000 in credit card debt.

Often people have a complicated relationship with money. How you acquire, spend and manage money can stem from your childhood influences (like parents, friends and the society you live in), what we learned from our mistakes and advice we are given from friends. I want to believe that most times people make good decisions when faced with a not so great financial situation. But sadly, many people don't even know how to handle them when they come. Your relationship with money provides the foundation for your spending habits; subsequently, dictating the choices and paths you take. Most people fit into five money personalities:

1. ***Spender***. The spender likes to enjoy themselves. They love to give gifts—sometimes these gifts can be extravagant. The spender also enjoys being the life of the party, and spending money comforts them. Sometimes this type of personality is known for trying to keep up with the Joneses.

2. ***Penny Pincher***. The penny pincher is the exact opposite of the big spender. They want to save every penny for an emergency, or a future purchase. This type of personality doesn't get to enjoy their money and live in the present very often. They typically have their budget down to the cent and can explain any variances.

3. ***Free Spirit***. The free spirit tends to have money come to them pretty easily. They may inherit it, win

it or merely earn it. This type of personality may think they can save everyone financially by funding other people's shortfalls. They will invest every dime in a dream. They are always looking for the big payoff and very unconcerned about what it takes to get there.

4. **Whiner**. The whiner is never at fault. It is always someone else's fault. They can never keep a full-time job—or for that matter, a part-time job. This type of personality still has their hands out, looking for someone to bail them out and pay for them. The whiner is not interested in setting up a financial plan.

5. **Guru**. The guru is the most even-tempered of all the personalities. They like to spend, save, invest and give when needed. They believe that their financial plan is like the Bible. It is a guide to how they should live their life. They are pretty savvy when it comes to their finances.

Understanding your money personality will help you pinpoint the areas you need to work on the most. Don't be surprised if you fit into two personality types—one will be your most dominant type.

Consider sharing your money personality with an accountability partner; who can help you identify behaviors you may need to change to reach your goals.

So, which money personality are you?

Accountability Partner

An accountability partner is a person who will help you stay on track with your overall goals. I have had several accountability partners during my lifetime, and I've learned along the way that there are specific characteristics you need to look for in a person before choosing them. These are your hopes and dreams we're talking about--not to mention your credit score! We can't entrust that stuff to just anyone. Let's discuss the characteristics you should look for during your selection process.

First, you have to share your financial goals and personal dreams with your accountability partner so they will know what to hold you accountable to. A good accountability partner must be:

1. ***Honest*** - your accountability partner has to be brutally honest with you without fear of reproach. This person will discuss with you whether they believe you're on target to reach your goals or not based on their own observations. For instance, if your goal is to save $1,000 by the end of the year, and its already September and you haven't saved a dime, but they see you with new clothes all the time, then their job is to wave the red flag. They need to be honest and tell you that you are not going to reach your goals unless you change your behavior.

2. ***Encouraging*** – your accountability partner needs to be supportive. We all need someone to pat us on the back when we're doing well and hold our hand when things aren't going so well. You need someone to celebrate your victories with, and someone to keep you on track when you're getting discouraged about your goals.

3. ***Compassionate*** – your accountability partner should be kind. You want to find someone that will show concern when you need it.

4. ***Good Listener*** – your accountability partner must be a good listener. They have to be able to hear what you're saying--and what you're *not* saying. How often do we hide what's really going on in our lives from our friends? If you are experiencing a hard time, you want that person to have a good listening ear and a deep level of discernment. It really helps to have someone who knows you well enough to pick up on when things aren't right.

5. ***Non-judgmental*** – your accountability partner should not be a judging person. The last thing you want in your life when you are trying to fix your finances is someone giving you the side-eye all of the time! And don't even think of choosing

someone you're afraid might talk about you behind your back. You should be able to tell this person anything, so take your time and choose wisely. Remember, if you feel judged by your partner, you won't feel safe being honest with them, and then the whole system falls apart.

I have plenty of experience in being an accountability partner. I've held that role for family members, friends and co-workers on several occasions. It's really what gave me the idea to start my own business. I was already offering advice and teaching people how to save and get out of debt. I was simply sharing with them how I overcame similar financial situations. As I mentioned before, who better to help you than someone who has gone through a financial situation, conquered it and found their way to financial fitness. Having a degree in accounting and business didn't hurt either. This would mark the beginning of Windsong Financial Coaching, LLC, a financial coaching business I created in 2017 to help women become financially fit one step at a time. I wanted women to understand how to own their financial destiny.

Don't feel like you have to take this financial journey alone. An accountability partner can help you through the challenging times. And there will be times you're going to want to revert back to your old spending habits. Reach out to a friend, but make sure it is someone you trust; because you will be sharing you're most personal thoughts and visions for your life.

Own Your Financial Destiny

"What we think, or what we know, or what we believe is, in the end, of little consequence. The only consequence is what we do."

~John Ruskin~

Chapter 4
Activate Your Vision

What is your '*Why*'? The reasons why we want to become financially fit differ with each person. Some save for their children's future, their first home, a car, or a dream vacation. Your why may even change the older you get. During this phase in my life, my "*Why*" includes several reasons—one of which is the quality of life I want for my family. Some others are funding my daughter's college education, taking care of my mom, funding my retirement and awesome vacations with my husband.

So, how can you discover your why? Write a list of the goals you want to accomplish that requires you to have good credit or a large sum of money. On a scale of 1 – 5, 5 being most important, rate each goal according to your level of passion for achieving that goal. After that, create a money mantra connected to that specific goal and BOOM! You have your why.

Here's an example of a money mantra: *I am capable of and looking forward to saving $5,000 to pay for next year's family vacation to Hawaii. We're going to have so much fun and I can't wait!* Your goal is to save $5,000 and your 'W*hy*' is to take your family to Hawaii for some fun, bonding, and quality time. Now, you try it.

The lesson here is, when you know your '*Why*', when you know what you're working towards, it's easier to build a budget, and you'll work harder to stick to it.

The all-powerful '*Why*' gives you a purpose, it is motivating, and it inspires you to work harder to reach your goals.

According to philosopher Friedrich Nietzsche, "a person who has a 'why' to live can tolerate almost any 'how.'" Not everything about sticking to your budget will be fun--even though it's been a blast so far, right? *Right*!

Just remember this: keeping your '*Why*' in mind will help you get through the hard times and stay on track in your quest for financial fitness.

Your Subconscious Can Work for Your Benefit

Your why can and will always reside in your subconscious, and may create thoughts like, *we don't need to eat out—buy groceries and cook at home*, or *instead of going to the movies, find a free one on Netflix*. That's right--the more you work at this, the more those good thoughts will kick in automatically. Believe it or not, your brain is on your side here.

Your subconscious will help you to focus on ways to save money, as opposed to spending frivolously. It's teaching you how to budget your money. Remember, your goal has been planted within your mind, so subconsciously, your actions will align with your goal.

Many people think saving money means you can't live and have fun when you want; so not true! Just because you're saving your money doesn't mean you can't live a good life. It's just the opposite: you can have as much fun as you want. In fact, I suggest you budget (uh oh there's that word people hate) for it, unless you have piles of money just laying around or growing on trees, in which case I'm coming over!

Plan to spend some money, a reasonable amount, no more than you can actually afford, on something fun every week. Budgeting helps you prepare for all of the what-ifs in life. It enables you to take one step closer to financial fitness. Don't worry!

I'll teach you how to budget in Chapter 7. Until then let's see what you are looking forward to in life.

Think Big

Imagine not having to stress about bills, debt, retirement or college for your children. Imagine not worrying about taking care of your elderly parents when that time presents itself. And when that vacation you've been looking forward to is finally here, you can actually relax without the stress of thinking about the bills that will be waiting for you back home. Basically, when your finances are in order, your quality of life gets better. Nice, right?!

Financial fitness is a possibility for everyone who has the mindset and willingness to work towards this goal. One of the ways you can keep your focus on becoming and staying financially fit is by creating a vision statement in each phase of your life.

A vision statement is a written inspirational description of what you want to accomplish at certain points in your life. So, what is your *vision statement* for this period in your life? Do you have one? If not it's pretty easy to put one together. Just spend a little time thinking about what you want. Write (or type) what you would like to accomplish and by when. Think big, and keep it short; two sentences at the most.

Implementing your vision statement will help you become more aggressive with your goals. First, post it somewhere you can see it every day. I post mine on the mirror in my bathroom, and on my computer at work. I even have it posted on my Facebook page. It reminds me of what I'm working towards. I have two vision statements, one for my business and another for my personal life. See them below:

Personal

Live to the fullest, Love will all your heart and Laugh as loud as you can.

Business

To Help Women Become Financially Fit One Step at a Time.

Next, I work out the how- *how I'm going to accomplish my vision.* I do this by creating S.M.A.R.T.E.R. goals.

Creating S.M.A.R.T.E.R Goals

Now that you have your vision statement posted and ready to keep you inspired, let's chat about another critical factor in becoming financially fit. You will need to set yourself up with a couple of S.M.A.R.T.E.R Goals. They will help you to actually reach that amazing vision that you've created for yourself. Many people equate their financial success to setting goals, and not just any goals—clear and concise goals.

On your journey to becoming financially fit, you must know what direction you're heading in and how you're going to get there. Setting S.M.A.R.T.E.R goals not only keeps you on track— but they'll also help you organize your time and effort. According to Tommy Brown, the author of **Seven Mindsets**, recent studies show only 20% of the population actually sets goals at all, and as many as 92% of those goals are never achieved.

> *"People with clear, written goals accomplish far more in a shorter period of time than people without them could ever imagine."*
>
> **~Brian Tracy~**

Okay, so by now you've probably figured out that you want to be in that 20% that sets goals, but how do you make sure your goals are part of the 8% that is achieved? The key to achieving goals is to be very detailed when writing them. Your goals should be motivating enough for you to keep pushing you forward even when you're ready to give up, as well as have enough depth to help you stay focused.

You should be passionate about your goals, and they should stretch your imagination. Don't create vague goals based on what you think others might expect you to want. Really put yourself into your goals! They are yours and nobody else's. Goals should tell you exactly what to do to reach your fantastic vision.

The term SMART goals have been around for a while. However, S.M.A.R.T.E.R. goal setting adds two more steps to the process, which help focus on evaluating and readjusting your goals. There may be times when your goals no longer work for you, this is the time to change them for the future. On the next page, I have added a S.M.A.R.T.E.R. goal setting chart with examples for you to review and use to start writing some of your own.

SMARTER GOAL EXAMPLE

I plan to save $1000 to purchase a new washing machine for my house.

I plan to save 20% of my paycheck for the next 5 weeks

I know I can save 20% of my paycheck because I just paid off my credit card bill which was the same amount.

This goal is very realistic, saving this money does not create any stress on my finances.

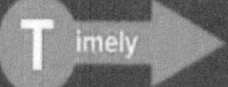
I plan to save this money monthly, with a deadline of 5 weeks from now (end of August).

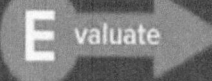
I will review my savings goal to make sure I am saving at the rate I planned.

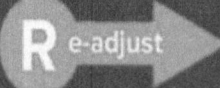
After my evaluation I find that I can no longer reach my desired goal, due to some circumstance, I will readjust my goal to a lower amount. I will not give up on my goal.

S.M.A.R.T.E.R. Goals must be:

- **Specific** - include who, what, where, when, and how you are going to accomplish your goals. You also have to do some soul-searching when setting your goals. If all you can think up is something vague and general, like "spend less" or "save more," you're going to need to break it down a little more. How many dollars less are you going to spend per week? What are you going to cut out or cut down on to save money? How much money are you going to set aside each week, and where are you going to put it? We need *details*.

- **Meaningful** - not just something you write on a piece of paper. Your goal should have a purpose. It should provide motivation, give you something to look forward to. Your goal should be firmly connected to your '*why*'.

- **A**chievable - the worst thing you can do is to set yourself up for failure by creating unachievable goals. Don't bite off more than you can chew at once, and don't ask the impossible of yourself. Also, make sure you've set a goal with a finite end--to do a specific thing by a particular time, or until you've reached a specific amount, so you'll actually know when you've achieved it. If you don't know when you've won, how can you celebrate?
- **Realistic** - You don't want to create a goal that doesn't stretch your imagination a little. However,

the goal shouldn't be too difficult to achieve. Setting goals aren't always easy—you have to dig deep and dream. Sometimes you may think that your ideas are too lofty, but if you can figure out a way to pull your ideas out of the clouds and create a plan to accomplish them, then congratulations-- you've just made your dreams a smart goal.

- ***Timely*** - Establish a timeframe for your goals. You don't want to give yourself years to accomplish a goal that you know you can complete in a couple of months. Likewise, you don't want to set your deadline for six months when you need more than a year. When you have finished listing a specific, meaningful, achievable and realistic goal, you need to assess your timeframe. You may not always be able to accomplish your goals as quickly as you'd like to, and that's okay. We can't control life. There may be situations that knock you off track temporarily, but having strong **S.M.A.R.T.E.R.** goals will help you to get back on quickly.

- ***Evaluate*** – Continue to evaluate your goals. Create a schedule to review them to make sure they are still in line with your vision. Sometimes we set goals and never take the time to adjust them when life changes. Your goals should make you stretch and keep you moving forward.

- ***Re-adjust*** – Lastly, you want to re-adjust your method of reaching your goal. If you are consistently not achieving your goals, it may be time to re-adjust your 'how'. Look at how you are trying to accomplish the goal, is it working for you? If not, find another way. You're not getting rid of the goal, you're just tweaking how you're going to reach the goal.

Goal setting is an integral part of life, and writing your goals down helps them to become tangible and actionable steps for you to follow. Creating goals also assist you with building a visual guide to help achieve your wildest dreams. S.M.A.R.T.E.R goals also allow us to establish metrics that can help us judge our progress.

"You must first know where you are before you can get to where you want to go."

~Felicia Petit-Frere~

Chapter 5
Acknowledge Your Current State

To know where you're going, you must know where you are, right? You would be amazed how many people have no idea what their current financial situation looks like. I admit it can be very scary, surprising, unbelievable, disappointing or even depressing when you really sit down and put it all on the table. I get it. It's stressful!

Those reactions are very normal, but you can't get stuck there. You have to get back on your feet and keep moving forward. You can only level up from here. What do I mean by level up? Good question! Level up means an increase in value or status. Take a couple of deep breaths, pour yourself a cup of tea, and get ready. We're about to level up!

Okay, now for the challenging part: let's look at the big picture. Take your time to research the answers; you will want a clear understanding of your financial story. Let's examine your current state by answering the following questions. Be honest when answering each question. The worst thing is to lie to yourself about where your finances are.

1. How much do you owe your creditors? Include mortgages, car payments, loans, credit cards, etc.

2. How much are your household utility bills?

3. Are all your bills current? If not, list the amount you're overdue on.

4. How much is your total income? How much is your net income?

5. Do you have enough income to pay your bills? If not, list three options that will help you earn more money.

6. Do you have a savings account? If so, how much are you saving each month? If you are not saving, why?

7. Have you pulled your credit score recently? What is it?

8. Do you have a monthly budget? If so, are you using it every month?

9. If you don't have a budget, what are you using to keep track of your spending?

Great, all the research is complete. Be sure to keep a notebook or a spreadsheet handy with your current financial numbers. This will help you track your progress and create a realistic plan of action. If you answered no to the second half of the questions on the previous page, these are the areas you need to work on.

For example, if you don't have a budget, now is the time to create one (Chapter 7 will help with that) and most importantly, follow it.

We will discuss debt in detail in a later chapter, but for now, try not to beat yourself up if you've made a few bad financial decisions—we all have honey, and it's okay!

At this point, you just need to recognize your mistakes, learn from them and push forward. Take this day and every day going forward to make more thoughtful decisions. Make sure you remember how you feel in this moment—this will inspire you to never put yourself back there again.

If your numbers didn't surprise you, then you've made good financial decisions. Keep up the good work! Continue reading, because I'm sure there is still something that can be improved to help you stay ahead of your finances.

In this financial game, you not only need to *R.O.C.K. Your Money*, honey—you have to work your credit, too. To know your current financial situation, you also need to understand your credit situation.

The Pretty Plastic

I gave credit cards a nickname: I call them the "pretty plastic"; it is quite pretty. Many credit card companies allow you to customize your credit cards by adding a personal picture on the front. You can use almost any picture you want, a beautiful picture of yourself, a scenic view, a picture of your dog, etc. Credit companies will go to any means to entice you to fall for the pretty plastic—trust me, I know. They even lure students in with free gifts (a t-shirt, a mug, or bag). As a college student, the word "free" is especially enticing when you're broke.

These companies *love* college students. When I attended college, one out of every four students left with at least one credit card. I quickly became a statistic; it was another way for me to live the life I wanted and pay for it later. The pretty plastic was my friend. What amazes me is that I was able to apply for and receive a credit card WITHOUT an INCOME.

Yes, you read it right; I did not have an income when I applied for my first credit card. I used my financial aid award as my income. I was approved within days, and the "Pretty Plastic" was sent to me by mail. I maxed it out and expected my mom to help me pay the balance. If we couldn't pay it, *oh well*, I thought, *I'll pay it when I can.* I didn't understand credit, nor did I comprehend the meaning of being delinquent on my credit cards.

I had no clue how it would affect my credit score in the future. I was living for the here and now. College students today have a little more protection. The *Card Act* of 2009 started requiring applicants under the age of twenty-one to have an income or a co-signer.

This act requires an age limit and income, but it still doesn't teach responsibility.

According to Sallie Mae's "How America Pays for College 2013" survey, 30% of undergraduates reported having a credit card and carrying an average balance of $747. Freshmen carried the highest balance, on average—$1,007.

Can you imagine how many college students graduate with not only student loan debt, but credit card debt and a 525-credit score? I can because I was one of them. What a way to be welcomed into your new and exciting world, upside down in debt.

"It's not your salary that makes you rich, it's your spending habits."

~Charles A. Jaffe~

Chapter 6
Account for Your Spending

C an you envision a world where everyone can see into the future? I think they call it clairvoyance. I'm not sure I would like it; give me a little bit of the unknown in my life. It would probably be a very dull world with no surprises. On the other hand, I don't want any surprises with my money! To alleviate the surprises, you must know what you're spending, write it down; create a spreadsheet; use an app or software. How you do it is not as important as finding the commitment to keep it up. You must do the work. In the end, you will have a clear picture of where your money is going.

According to an article in Business Insider, 61% of Americans do not track their spending. You know what that tells me? 61% of Americans have absolutely no clue what they are spending. It's sad to say, but they don't know where their money is going. It's as if they just threw their money out the window with nothing to show for it.

Do you fall into this category? If you feel like this is your story, I'd like to teach you how to account for your spending. Here's an exercise that will be helpful to you:

1. **Know where your money is going** - You want to be in control of your finances, use the same exercise I gave one of my clients. Start tracking your expense using a journal/notebook or a spreadsheet (see page 49 for an example). Select a timeframe (it can be weekly or monthly) to review your list. If you are overspending, this is the time to adjust your habits.

2. **Gauge how close you are to reaching your goals** - Comparing your spending to your **S.M.A.R.T.E.R.** goals (created in Chapter 4) allows you to see the full picture. Let's say one of your goals is to save up for a down payment on your dream home by a specific date. This comparison will help you gauge whether you are on target to reach your goals.

3. **Learn how to prioritize your spending** - If something is not helping you get closer to your goals ask yourself, *do I really need this*? I'm not saying take all of the fun out of your life, but if you are trying to pay off debt wasting money is only going to cost you more in the long run.

4. **Become more aware of your spending habits** - Tracking your spending makes all of your spending habits plain and clear. You can't ignore a $300 Starbucks habit if it is on the page staring you right in the face.
5. **Be aware of erroneous charges** - There are some terrible people in the world that believe their job is to steal your money. Reviewing your bank statement and tracking your spending helps pinpoint erroneous charges.

On the next page, I have included a copy of the spreadsheet I use, as well as my clients, to track our spending. You can use whatever you like, it's simply a way to track your spending. Remember, this exercise helps you acknowledge your current state.

Use bank statements, they should have all of your expenses listed. Make sure to include *every* expense for the month, even the small items you don't think matters. This method will not work if you omit expenses.

R.O.C.K Your Money Expense Tracker

Expenses	Category	Amount

Chapter 7

Assemble Your Budget

I remember sitting with a client drifting in and out of the conversation. I was thinking to myself, *when is she going to get off this merry go round?* I know that was horrible for me to do, but I'm also human. As a kid, it's fun to hop on and off the playground ride, but as an adult, it's just insanity. She continues to do the same thing every payday, but she expects different results.... sounds like insanity to me. Have you found yourself on the same financial merry go round? If so, it's time to jump off! Just jump. Don't be afraid to scrape your knee, it will heal. Get up and brush yourself off and get ready to meet your goals. At least that's what I told her, I had to warn her that she was going down a road that was about to dead end right into a pitfall of debt.

Does this remind you of your own money story? At one point in my life, this was me. I realized I wasn't going to make it very far if I kept up that behavior. I asked my client to list all of the items she spent money on in the prior month. Guess what? She couldn't do it! She could not tell me where her money went during the month. I gave her an assignment. Heck yeah, I gave her homework. She asked for help now it was time to do the work. She had to track her spending during the month in a journal she carried with her at all times. I didn't want her to forget anything, including the gourmet coffee she purchased every morning on her way to work.

When we met the next week, she had her list ready to review, but she wasn't happy about the outcome. We realized she spent over $80 on Starbucks coffee a month. She had a specific morning routine that she followed, and if she didn't have her coffee her day wouldn't be the same.

Subconsciously she knew her routine was too expensive, but she told herself that everyone has that one guilty pleasure. When we finished with her list, she had about five guilty pleasures worth $300 a month. Crazy, right? When we first started, she had no idea where her money was going.

During our session, we were able to create a very manageable budget. I'm happy to say that she still follows her budget and has been able to burn down over 30% of her debt.

Financial knowledge is empowering, just think about it. When you set strong goals, and create a plan to accomplish them... life feels great! You almost feel like you can do anything.

We have reviewed a majority of the steps needed to put your financial plan together, now it's time to create it.

In the next section, we will discuss wants vs. needs. I will share my signature step-by-step technique - The LEAP Method, designed to help you create a realistic plan of action. Don't forget to add in your "small wins" for encouragement. It can be hard to stick to a plan, so celebrating your little victories gives you a little something to look forward to along the way.

Assess Your Wants vs. Needs

It's the good old wants versus needs conversation. I know we all hate to have it because some of us think we need it all. Of *course*, I need my luxury car with seat warmers. Believe it or not it gets cold in the south. Sounds funny, doesn't it? But that's how we think. Have you ever heard of the saying, "it's a thin line between love and hate?" Well, I guarantee the line is even thinner between a want and a need.

How many times have you gone to the mall intending to purchase a few items and left with more than you needed? At the check-out, you look at your receipt wondering what the heck you bought. At the time, your purchase seemed like a necessity, you used your 20% off coupon, so you feel like you saved money on the purchase. We've all done it, for some people shopping is therapeutic. For others going shopping- when you don't need to- is just a bad decision. In either case, the purchase is not a necessity.

There are only four things you need for basic survival. I know it's a bit of a generalization, but here they are:

1. *A roof over your head*
2. *Enough food and water to maintain your health*
3. *Basic health care and hygiene products*
4. *Clothing (just what you need to remain comfortable and appropriately dressed)*

Anything that goes above and beyond these four basic needs is a want. Does that mean you shouldn't enjoy the finer things in life? Absolutely not, but it does mean that you need to be selective in the things that you purchase. For instance, let's say you just celebrated your birthday, and as luck may have it everyone gave you money. Since you have extra money you thought about paying on some of your overdue bills, but your urge to splurge over powered your financially savviness. Sure, you looked great with your new purchase, but did you really need it?

Likewise, before making large purchases, or spending the money that's burning a hole in your pocket think of how much time you spent working to make it. For example, if you make $20 per hour and you spend $40 to go out and eat, you just spent two hours' worth of work. Does that sound like a waste? By effectively converting the monetary figure to an hourly one, it can serve to deter you from making purchases you might regret, which can help combat impulsive spending.

I'm not saying you can't splurge and have fun sometimes. What I am saying is be intentional with your money. Create a budget for those nights out on the town. Make sure you are not living paycheck to paycheck.

Let's discuss a couple of factors that contribute to the blurry line that most people draw between their needs and wants. Sometimes you may have a desire for something so great that you begin to make justifications as to why you should have it. Others feel a sense of entitlement to the better things in life because they have reached a certain status. Have you ever heard of the saying "Keeping Up with the Joneses"?

As adults, we often like to compare what we have with our friends, family, and neighbors. This type of thinking can get you into trouble if you aren't content with your life. If you can afford to pay for your wants without sacrificing a necessity, then I say, enjoy your money. However, if you are living off of your credit cards, stop now and ask for help.

How often do you get a "want" confused with a "need"? I know, I know we don't really want to think about it because "We Want What We Want When We Want it." Sometimes you feel like every shiny object is a need. Designer clothes, the hottest shoes, eating out—you just want it all. Name brand clothing, shoes and food *are* basic necessities, right? Wrong! Having a specific name brand on your clothes and shoes is a want, not a need; eating out is also a want. One of the biggest mistakes you can make is justifying a want into a need and not being prepared for the cost that comes with it.

It's okay to treat yourself along the way, but if you can't afford it, then it's okay to wait. Focusing on the difference between your wants and needs can help you to make better decisions, like saving more for the big-ticket items on your wish list. If it's vital, then create a plan to get it. You can be the person who makes it happen.

Now that you've had an honest conversation with yourself about your wants and needs, and created S.M.A.R.T.E.R. goals it's time to act on them. Putting together a plan, or should I say budget, may take a little while to accomplish. However, it will give you a sense of empowerment because you're working towards your own goals.

The next time you crave something that you can't afford, don't feel deprived. Assess whether it's a want or a need and whether it's in alignment with your goals. Trust me, it will make it easier to ignore those things that may get you off track.

The L.E.A.P. Method

To create your budget, or plan, we're going to use my signature exercise that I refer to as the L.E.A.P. method. This technique will teach you how to get down to the real deal, be honest, put everything on the line and assemble your plan. Implementing this process will initiate an honest discussion with yourself about your monthly expenses. It's okay to talk to yourself every once in a while.

The L.E.A.P method is designed to help you assess your current lifestyle and finances. I created this method to give my clients the ability to evaluate and categorize their expenses.

To use this method, you will need your list of expenses from page 69. Add four boxes on the right side of the spreadsheet. At the top of each column place an L, E, A, and P. There is an example of the *Let's L.E.A.P.* method on page 79. Review each of your expenses listed and check the appropriate box located on the right. The acronym for the L.E.A.P method is detailed below:

L - List all of your necessary expenses. These are expenses that you will keep, such as rent, mortgages, and utilities to name a few.

E - Eliminate unnecessary expenses these may be expenses you splurge on, but really can't afford. They are also expenses that you can eliminate immediately such as subscriptions, cable, or magazines.

A - Adjust the cost of expenses where you can. For example, maybe you don't need the NFL ticket; by taking it off of your cable bill you can lower your payment by $150.

P- Push these expenses to a later date when you can afford them. These are expenses that are considered nice to have, but you can't currently afford them, so you push them off to a later time frame.

After categorizing all your expenses, use the **L.E.A.P.** method summary on page 80 to calculate the total expenses you will ***Leave***- these are the expenses you will place on your budget spreadsheet, ***Eliminate***- these are the expenses you will get rid of, ***Adjust***- these are expenses you will decrease, or ***Push***- these are expenses you will stop purchasing until you can really afford them.

Lets L.E.A.P

Expenses	Category	Amount	L	E	A	P

Summarize Your Plan

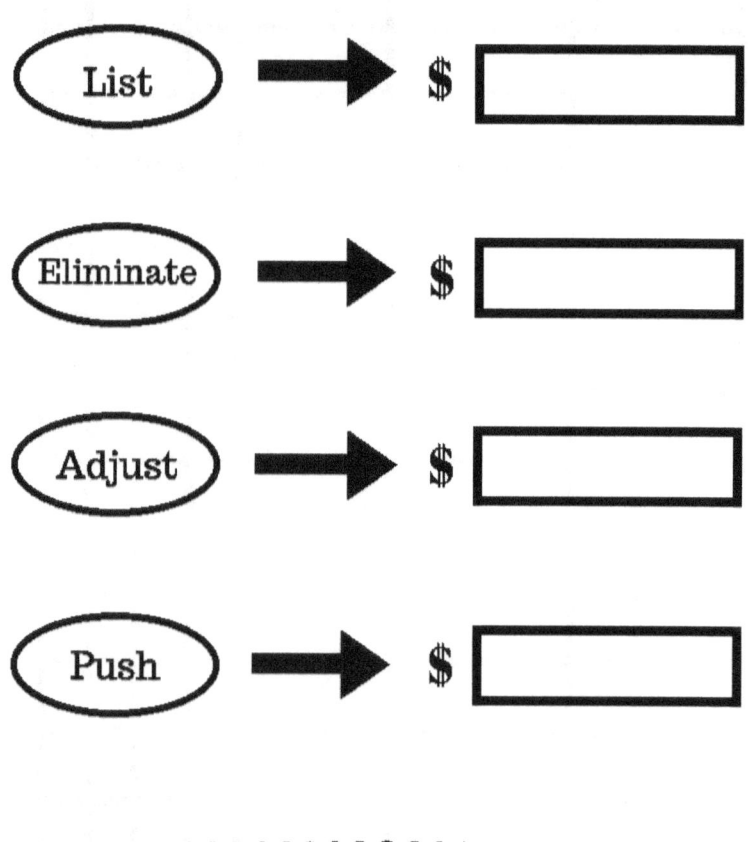

Create Your Budget

This is where the fun begins: it's time to create your budget. You're probably thinking, "Coach Fe is such a nerd." Well, you might be right; I love numbers, especially when they are working in my favor, and that's what a budget helps you to accomplish. I'm sure you can think of a million things that you want to do right now and creating a budget is not one of them.

Remember, we have already done the majority of the work with the L.E.A.P exercise. I wouldn't steer you wrong, this is the easy part. Sticking to your budget, now that's that hard part.

I often tell my clients, if you don't take time to tell your money where to go, you will wonder where it went. Now let's create the master plan- your budget. I have listed below some guidelines and percentages that can be followed when setting up your budget.

Windsong
Financial Coaching LLC

20%	Housing
15%	Transportation
15%	Life Insurance
10%	Healthcare
10%	Utilities
10%	Groceries
10%	Entertainment
10%	Savings

These numbers represent a percentage of your net income. There are two essential items that you need to know: your net income and your expenses. If you're lucky, your net income will exceed your expenses. If it doesn't, you're upside down, negative, this is not where you want to be. Believe it or not, some people base their spending on their total income. It is essential to understand this. I call it the formula; your net income is:

Net Income = Total Salary - Withholdings - Deductions (Also, add any additional income you receive).

Once you determine what your net income is, subtract your savings, investments, and all expenses. What you have left is yours to spend.

Creating a budget can be very simple. I teach my clients to K.I.S.S their budget, which stands for Keep It Sort of Simple. I know that sounds funny, but it works, and it will help you keep track of your expenses. It will also make the whole process a little more manageable. You need to see the big picture that your finances create. There are several different ways you can create your budget.

1. *You can use good old-fashioned pen and paper. I call this the manual budget.*
2. *You can create an Excel spreadsheet. This requires a little tech-savviness.*
3. *You can use an app such as Every Dollar and YNAB just to name a few. These apps set up everything for you.*

For starters, say I created my budget using a computerized spreadsheet. Next, I would add my expenses from my spending tracker (created on page 69). I would keep the expenses on my **Leave** list, delete the expenses on my **Eliminate** list, change the dollar amounts on the expenses I plan to **Adjust** and make a note of the expenses I'm **Pushing** to a future date. These expenses make up your monthly budget.

Take one more look at your spreadsheet to ensure everything is accurate and up to date. Don't forget to compare your expenses to the percentage of net income chart on page 84. It may take a little time to fall in line with those percentages, but at least you have a guideline. Add a column for your budgeted amount, actual amount, and due date if you like (see example on page 85).

You can also take your budget a little farther by categorizing your expenses into fixed and variable.

- ***Fixed expenses*** – these are your rent, mortgages, car payments and any other expenses that are the same amount each month.
- ***Variable expenses*** – these are your utility bills, credit cards, gas, groceries, and any other expenses that change month to month.

If you really want to become a pro at budgeting, you can add another subcategory. For instance, if you have a fixed and variable section, you can list credit cards under variable, and under fixed you can list mortgages/rent.

Expenses that fluctuate month to month can be estimated by using the average of the last six months. Put it all together, and you have a budget. At the end of each month, review your detailed budget and create a summary. Don't beat yourself up if you stray every once in a while. Just pick it back up and get back on track. There is an example on the follow page.

Net Income $_____

Expenses $_____

Savings $_____

Investments $_____

Play Money $_____

The PLAN/ BUDGET
(Month 1)

Expense Item	Budget	Actual Exp.
Subtotal		

Income 1

Income 2

Other Income

Total Income

Savings

Actual Exp.

Remaining Bal

Sometimes we need a reminder of where we are and where we want to be. If paying off expenses to increase your credit score or to just simply save more is one of your goals, I have something special for you in the next section. I'll teach you how to burn down your debt using two simple, yet effective methods. But for now, let's get back to creating your budget. Remember, pay yourself (by depositing at least 10% of your net income into your savings) first. Don't even think about it, automate it.

Automate Savings

Have you ever known anyone who couldn't keep a dollar in their pocket to save their life? Maybe their money was burning a hole in their pockets, or perhaps they just didn't have enough discipline to save.

According to a survey conducted by GoBankingRates, 45% of Americans are living paycheck to paycheck. Yep, they just can't hang on to their money. Some may think if they could just make more money, all their problems would be solved. However, 1 in 10 people making over $100,000 a year says they still live paycheck to paycheck. I am here to tell you that if you lack discipline, it doesn't matter how much money you make—you will always spend more than you save.

Finding Your Discipline

Many people lack the discipline needed to save just because their mind is always focused on the next purchase. Have you ever thought to yourself, "Where did my money go?"

Well, let's see. You may have gone to the store for a pair of shoes, but when you left the store you had shoes, a dress, and a new purse. Welcome to the life of an impulsive spender.

To combat impulsive spending, you MUST practice being intentional with your money. If your employer is still paying you with a paper check, you may want to ask about direct deposit. Each payday your check will automatically be deposited directly into your bank account, this will help you reduce the amount of money you spend.

When your paycheck is deposited into your bank account, set up an automatic transfer to move at least 10% (to start) to your savings account. This method is called *Paying Yourself First.* If you can afford it, I recommend setting up an emergency fund with at least a six-month cushion. If you can't save six months, then save as much as you can. After paying yourself, pay everyone else by setting up automatic recurring bill payments for things like- your mortgage, utilities, car payment, investments, insurance, and credit cards.

When your savings is funded and your monthly bills are taken care of, the rest is free for you to spend on whatever you want.

Let's Burn Some Debt

If you have gotten this far, you should be proud of yourself! You have created a realistic budget and made a commitment to follow it, now it's time to do the work. Yes, it's time to burn that debt!!! Can you tell I am your biggest cheerleader? I have been under a mountain of debt and dug my way out, so I know it can be done. I know the feeling of making that last payment, it is an absolutely fabulous feeling! It's a clean slate, the point at which your new goals and dreams can start to flourish. Have I encouraged you enough? I sure hope so! Now let's chat about two methods you can use to burn debt.

Method 1: The Debt Snowball

I know, the name sounds funny, but the method works. It reminds of me of some of the snowy winters I had growing up in Richmond, VA. I loved being at my Grandmother Mildred's house because we would go outside and have snowball fights. There was a process to making the best snowballs. You would start with a small amount of snow to make your ball and keep adding more snow to make it bigger and bigger. Once you have that nice, big snowball, you're ready to throw it at the first person you see....... BAM! Hits the person in the back. That was so much fun.

A debt snowball is created the same way, only this time you're using your bills instead of snow. The first step is to use the list of debt you created before (do not include your mortgage or car payment), beside each bill write your minimum payment. Then put your bills in order (smallest to largest) by account balance. Now you can start the snowball process. Let's began creating the ball.

Start by paying as much as you can on your smallest bill, while paying the minimum payment on your remaining bills. Continue this step until you pay off your first bill. The next month you will use the money you gained (from paying off your first bill) plus the minimum you were paying on your next smallest bill. Continue paying on this bill while paying the minimums on your remaining accounts until they are all paid off. Now you have created your snowball, and you can see it getting bigger and bigger....... BAM! You are knocking those bills out.

I know what you're thinking; this method is going to cost you because you're not paying off the higher balances first. Well, you are correct, but one thing we know as Americans, we like things to happen quickly.

Paying off smaller bills gives us quick victories, and you'll need them to stay motivated on your financial journey. Think about it, when you pay off a balance on your list it makes you feel good. Then you pay off the next smallest balance you feel even better. You're now committed, and you can see the plan working. Now you're well on your way to *Rocking Your Money Story* and reaching one of your goals: becoming debt-free.

Still concerned about not paying those higher balances off first? Keep reading I have something for you, too.

Method 2: The Debt Avalanche

I can't say that I have ever experienced a real avalanche, but I can tell you a debt avalanche is a compelling debt payoff method. Unlike the debt snowball, the debt avalanche method starts with the highest interest first then down to the lowest. You will use the same list you used in the debt snowball, but instead of listing your minimum payments you will record the interest rate for each bill. Next, put them in order by interest rate, largest to smallest.

Start by paying as much as you can on your highest interest bill, while paying the minimum payment on your remaining bills. Continue this step until you pay off your first bill. The next month you will use the money you gained (from paying off your first bill) plus the minimum you were paying on your future highest interest. Continue paying on this bill while paying the minimums on your remaining accounts until they are all paid off.

The little victories will not come as quickly, but if you know anything about interest, when you pay your balance down, the less interest you have to pay.

Can you see the avalanche now? If you remain dedicated to this method, your debt will be wiped away in time, just be patient.

The work does not stop here, your next step is to audit and adjust your plan.

You can't change the past, but you can adjust the present for the future.

~Unknown~

Chapter 8
Audit and Adjust Your Plan

When you commit to your financial plan, you must remember it is an ongoing process. Don't create it, commit to it, and then forget it. Stick with it! Often times, people tend to think they can build a budget and leave it. The worst thing is realizing a year later that you haven't had much progress in achieving your goals because you didn't audit your progress and make adjustments when needed. This is why I created the audit and adjust step.

Let's review an example of the audit and adjust step. You decided that enough is enough, you are tired of the debt and ready to get a fresh start. We look at your current state, I recommend different methods you can use. You chose the snowball method and started paying off your debt. Somewhere along the way, you increased some of your expenses. For instance, the cable bill increased, because you added more channels. Your utility bill fluctuated because of the season, and your mortgage changed because of an increase in real-estate taxes. But you did not adjust your budget to reflect the changes. Keep in mind, you must audit and adjust your finances to cover the additional expenses, or you may experience a failed budget. Auditing and adjusting your budget for any changes is the key to maintaining a balanced budget.

Be Humble and Patient

Being able to humble yourself is a necessary characteristic on your journey to *ROCK Your Money*. Don't be afraid to ask for help. As women, we are sometimes concerned about what people think of us. At this point, what others think is not very important. In fact, my next client, had to learn the hard way when she and her family had no choice but to move in with her in-laws.

The bill collectors were calling, they couldn't pay the mortgage on their dream home, they were behind on their credit card bills and started bouncing checks. SHE WAS STRESSED....pushed past her limits. They had no clue how much they owed anyone, they just knew it was a lot, and they didn't want to rob Peter to pay Paul anymore. She and her husband had to sit down, focus, and rebuild. They were so disappointed in themselves and didn't want anyone to know what they were going through, they didn't want to ask anyone for help. It took them a little time to grasp being humble enough to let someone help them.

I repeatedly talked to them about the importance of auditing their finances each month and adjusting their budget if needed. My client and her husband had already gone through my financial program, and they were doing very well.

Or so I thought.

One day, after they had been in the program for a while, they started noticing extra money in their account. At this point they had paid off some of their expenses. Needless to say, the extra money created a false sense of security for them, and they fell back into the same practices that initially caused their financial issues, spending money on the more beautiful things in life. Neither of them was reviewing the finances to make sure they didn't spend more than they could afford.

They ended up underwater again because neither wanted to cut back on the expenses. They were busy trying to keep up with the Joneses and worrying about what their friends would say. When they realized there was a problem they wanted a quick fix so no one would know what they were going through.

After loading on the debt again they decided it was time to give me a call. During our first session, I had them look up and learn the definition of the word patience. According to Webster's dictionary, patience is the ability to remain calm and not become annoyed when waiting for a long time, or when dealing with problems. You may be thinking, *why did she have them look up that word?* Well, what's the first thing people think about when they start having financial problems?

They wanted their financial problems fixed quickly, and unfortunately that wasn't going to happen. Some people think there is a magical wand that they can wave and all their financial woes will disappear. When you find this wand please send me one. Fixing financial issues and teaching someone how to manage their money definitely doesn't happen overnight- it takes time.

Truth is, we all have moments of weakness. I probably had a good five years of weakness. I also had to learn how to be patient with my own process. I learned that along with having patience, there were three other important things I had to remember:

1. *Humble yourself and ask for help*
2. *Audit your budget*
3. *Make adjustments if needed*

Auditing and adjusting your budget on a regular basis will help you stay on track. We all know that unexpected things, good and bad, can happen at the most inopportune time. Case in point, you may receive a raise at work, or your car may break down. You want to make sure you keep the issues you can't control to a minimum, like spending too much money at the mall.

If you know shopping is a big temptation, stop spending your spare time at the mall or wherever you shop the most. I know.... It's easier said than done. I love to shop, too, but wasting money has never helped me reach any of my goals. I can't put enough emphasis on the importance of auditing your budget.

To help you stay on track with this routine, set up specific timeframes to audit and make adjustments to your budget if necessary. Decide if you want to audit monthly, bi-monthly or quarterly; it's up to you. I suggest beginners audit and adjust monthly. This allows you to take time and reflect back to the start of the year or when you originally created your budget. You'll be able to see if you've fallen short of your financial goals. If your life took an unexpected turn, you may need to re-evaluate your goals at this time.

Now that you're clear on *why* you should audit your budget, let's discuss *how* to perform an audit. Start your audit by downloading your monthly bank statements and label each transaction. Do that for two months and then compare the current month to the prior month by completing the following:

1. Audit and compare your recurring payments.
2. Add a note for each variance to explain the expense.
3. Add a note to explain any new transactions on your statement.

4. Review all of your transactions and make adjustments where needed.

This process may be a bit overwhelming the first time. Make a promise to yourself, your vision and goals that you will succeed. Also, by auditing, you may be able to save a little more money by identifying unhealthy financial habits, such as unnecessary spending and splurging.

Create Your Own Money Story

"Your money story is just like any other story in a book, you need to know how you want it to begin and end".

~Coach Fe~

Chapter 9
The Power of Three Little Numbers

Mariyah had been working at her dream job for a solid year, today was her work anniversary, and she knew exactly how she was going to celebrate. You see, every day after work Mariyah would stop by the car lot and visit her new car, yes, she had already claimed it in her head. She had been saving for a while, and finally had enough for a nice down payment. Today she wasn't just going to visit her car, she was going to ride off the lot with it. She was very excited.

Mariyah had made plans to meet the salesman at 5:00 pm after work and she was right on time. They spent some time running her credit. Mariyah could already see herself in the car. However, this wouldn't happen. Mariyah wasn't able to purchase the car because she had a 565-credit score, which put her interest rate on the high end and made her monthly payment more than she could afford. She felt like she had let down one of the most important person in her life: herself.

How can one little three-digit number have so much power? Well, it gives lenders insight into how you handle your money. That little three-digit number represents you when you're not even in the room. It reflects the likelihood that you will repay your debts.

You may want to pull your credit report before you start the next section. You can request one free credit report from www.AnnualReport.com per year. Remember, this request will not include your credit score; that's extra.

Understanding Your Credit Report

Okay, let's have a truth moment: if you want to borrow money from any sort of financial establishment (except a payday loan company), your credit report must be reviewed. Your credit report gives the lender a snapshot of your financial history and may be accessed by potential employers, lenders and department stores. The information in your credit report determines your credit score. Understanding how to read your credit report, what comprises it and how to monitor it will help you handle your finances overall.

The three major credit bureaus are Equifax, Transunion, and Experian. Each of these bureaus collects information from public records and companies you do business with. They report your information in four categories: personal information, credit history, public records, and credit inquiries.

There are also three types of credit: mortgage, installment, and revolving. You want to keep your revolving credit below 30%.

Periodically review your entire report, but mostly focus on your credit history. Your credit history includes current and historical information on your credit card accounts, medical bills and your record of payment. When there is an error in reporting, you'll need to contact the company via a dispute letter.

You can also dispute through the credit bureaus, but you won't have documentation. Remember, check your credit at least once a quarter or more if you are very active credit card user. Use the chart below to find your credit score range.

If your credit score is categorized as fair or below, you need to spend some time focusing on improving your score.

Windsong
Credit Score Range
(FICO CLASSIC AND FICO 8 - RANGE 300-850)

Excellent	780-850
Very good	740-779
Above average	720-739
Average	680-719
Below average	620-679
Poor	580-619
Very poor	520-579
Worst	<520

Credit reports reflect how well you take care of your finances. Sometimes this is the only story that a creditor might see before deciding on your creditworthiness. Think about it—when you apply for credit a majority of the time it's an online application. You're not there to plead your case or discuss with the creditors your reasoning for falling behind or not making your payment. They don't really care that you could not pay your bill because your rent was due or you fell behind on your utility bills. Your creditors want to be paid by any means necessary. You can make a credit statement, but most creditors do not review that section of your credit report.

The Credit Scoring System

The most common credit scoring system used is the FICO score. FICO is an acronym for Fair Isaac Corporation. Most financial institutions use FICO because of the standard scoring system that they have created. Often people are baffled by the way their FICO score is calculated. I understand it can be very confusing.

There are five components used in the calculation of your FICO score.

1. **Payment History**
   Your payment history makes up 35% of your total credit score, making this the most critical factor in your credit score. FICO pays very close attention to whether you pay your bills on time.

Lesson: Make sure you pay your bills on time.

2. **Amounts Owed**
   The total amount owed to your creditor represents 30% of your overall credit score. This factor takes into consideration your credit utilization, meaning how much of your credit limit you're actually using. Are you maxing out your credit cards? There is no perfect number—it's different for each credit card. However, I believe if you keep your spending percentage to 30% of your limit or below, you'll be in a sweet spot.

   Lesson: Do not max out your cards.

3. **Length of Credit History**
   Your length of credit history represents 15% of your total credit score. This component tracks how long you've had credit. The longer your credit history, the better. Closing out your credit cards can cause your credit score to decrease because that history is no longer on your file. For those who have a shorter credit history, continue to be good stewards of your credit and time will be a positive factor for your credit history.

   Lesson: Do not close out your credit cards unless it is absolutely mandatory.

4. **New Credit**
   New credit represents 10% of your total credit score. You have to have credit to have a credit history. However, I encourage you to be careful with opening too much credit. Opening too many credit accounts within a short period of time may

raise a red flag. The credit bureaus may see this as a risk. New credit accounts will decrease your average length of credit history.

Lesson: Do not apply for credit cards you don't need.

5. Credit Mix

Your credit mix represents 10% of your total credit score. It evaluates your ability to handle payment of all types of credit. For instance, you could have a home mortgage, car loan, and two credit cards. This represents different kinds of credit, and lenders believe that consumers with several types of loans are less risky.

Lesson: It is essential to have more than one type of credit account. However, if you are not responsible enough to handle different types, just stick to one. If you are a visual person like

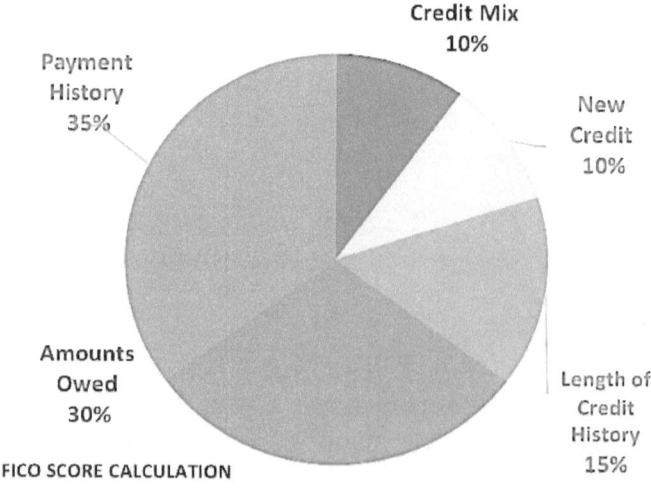

I am, see the pie chart below for an illustration.

Confusing enough right? Now that you know how each part of your FICO score is evaluated, I hope you have a better understanding of where you should focus your attention. You are the CEO of your own destiny, and you have total control over your credit score. You can choose to take care of it and ensure it represents you well, or you can be irresponsible—and your score will represent that, too.

Having a credit card is a huge responsibility, let me say this again - having a credit card is a huge responsibility and should not be taken lightly. If you know you're not responsible enough to handle a credit card, I strongly suggest not applying for one. I know it's tempting to feel like you need a card for emergencies, but in the end, you'll be setting yourself up for failure. Remember, credit does not equal free money!

In addition to understanding your credit score, you will want to know which credit score is being pulled for review. Yes, there is more than one type of credit score. I know, it's bad enough we have to keep track of our score, but do we really need to understand how all of them work? Well, let me ease your mind right now—you don't really need to know how they all work; you just need to see the importance of each of them.

Earlier in this chapter, we mentioned the most common credit scoring system used is the FICO score, but there are over 50 versions available. It just depends on who is requesting the information.

A car dealer may receive a slightly different score than a department store. Some lenders also base their decisions on the Vantage credit scoring model.

The Vantage Score is a product of credit bureaus: Experian, Equifax, and TransUnion. Vantage uses a credit score range of 300 to 850 to classify you.

A score of 690 and up is generally a good credit score. A score of 760 and above is considered excellent. A good to excellent credit score gives lenders the confidence in you and your ability to repay your debt. Your score provides the lender with a sense of your character (how you pay your bills) before they even take your first payment. Your job is to give the lender no reason to second guess you, that's if you use credit; some people don't. A simple drop in your credit score can cost you a lot of money.

5 Things That Will Lower Your Score

A drop in your credit score is definitely not a surprise you want to have. Luckily, you have the power to protect your score. You can avoid the five most significant things that can cause less-than-great credit if you know what they are, what they can do to your credit score and how your finances are affected when they appear on your credit report.

Generating Too Many Inquiries. Every time you apply for loans/credit cards, sign up for service contracts, even apply for jobs you are generating inquiries on your credit report. Some of these inquiries can negatively affect your credit rating, lenders check your credit report to assess how well you'll be able to pay off a loan or make regular payments on a service (these inquiries are called hard inquiries).

The more creditors check your file, the more it looks like you're trying to get credit all over the place. This can make you seem like more of a risk to potential lenders, the same way that you wouldn't feel great lending money to a friend who already owes money all over town. Hard inquiries can lower even a great credit score by five whole points. Ideally, you have to control the number of inquiries that will reflect on your credit history. Keep track of your credit applications to avoid the negative impact on your credit score.

Ignoring Unpaid Bills. When third-party agencies start contacting you to collect an unpaid debt, this is a significant indication for delinquency – or in other words, you've got a reputation for not paying your creditors back. Ignoring unpaid bills is never a wise thing to do, as this can lead to more serious problems: the debt can grow, collectors will keep calling you, you could be sued, your credit applications can get denied, your credit will suffer, the lenders may contact other people you know, and it can cause you a lot of stress. Knowing you have an unpaid bill might feel stressful enough that it feels more natural just to avoid it altogether, but facing the problem head-on is the only way to solve it.

Your unpaid bills are very much your responsibility, and your liability. When companies get tired of asking you to pay for your credit, they let debt collectors' step in to do the job for them. Once these third-party agencies report your unpaid bills to credit bureaus, your credit score will drop. Ignoring your bills won't make them go away, but it will make them cost you more in the long run.

Inaccurate Public Records. The public records section of your credit report includes details anyone can see if they look you up. For example, bankruptcies, tax liens, and civil judgments - all of which can harm your credit score if the information is accurate. However, sometimes a credit agency may report inaccurate information or keep an item on your report longer than seven years. I suggest reviewing your credit report quarterly, this way you can find and dispute inaccurate information. The last thing you want is to pay for financial mistakes you didn't even make!

Using Over 30% of Your Credit Line. If you are using over 30% of your credit line, you have more debt than recommended and less available credit. The less-than-30% rule has been tagged as a myth several times. It is a guideline, but it's a critical one which can save a high credit score from dropping. Maxing out your cards every month can suggest to creditors that you're living paycheck to paycheck, which means even if you're making your payments now, any sudden financial hardship that comes along could sink you.

It might give your creditors a wrong impression, but it's also *true*. If you're using your entire credit limit or a significant chunk of it, every single month, you probably aren't spending wisely. When you avoid using more than 30% of your available credit, it means that you are more aware and in control of your credit spending. It also implies that you're living safely within your means. It looks better to creditors—and it also looks better for your bottom line.

Having No Credit at All. Having no credit at all seems great in a way. If you're not borrowing anything, you're only spending your own money, so of course you're fiscally responsible, right? Maybe, but it doesn't look that way to creditors. Remember, your credit score determines the rates offered to you when you sign up for contracts and spend on big-ticket items that you want and need, like renting or buying a house, getting a car or insurance. If you don't have credit at all, companies won't be able to make a calculated prediction on how are you capable of managing your finances. Applying for a loan or a mortgage without any credit history is a lot like applying for a job without any work history.

As stated before, your credit report is like your resume – it proves that you've borrowed money before and that you've been able to pay it back. Paying for everything in cash might be responsible for you on an individual level, but it does nothing to prove that you're creditworthy. Maintaining good credit can be hard with the enticing offers that come with applying for credit. However, if you are trying to increase your credit score, you want to stay away from hard inquiries. Keep in mind that your credit is like your personality it tells lenders what type of person you are before they get to know you.

Don't Believe the Hype, It's Just a Myth

A little white lie never hurt anyone. It's an old saying, but people still live by it. Personally, I say a lie is a lie and don't care who tells it. Sometimes people dress it up and call it a myth. A myth is still not true no matter how you make it sound. Let's talk about some lies, I mean myths, that have been made up about credit. Don't believe everything you're told. Poor financial knowledge can hurt you, especially if you believe the stuff that has been passed down over the years. My top five credit myths are below:

1. *When you pay your credit cards off you should close them.* This credit myth recommends closing old accounts after they are paid off. Absolutely not; instead of closing the account, put the card away and don't use it. Closing an account is the quickest way to hurt your credit score. One of the most critical elements in calculating your credit score is the proportion of total balances to the overall credit limits.

2. *If I check my credit, my score will drop.* This myth makes people believe that every time they review their own score, their credit score drops. This is not the case. When you check your own score, there is no impact. However, as we learned above, if a *lender* checks your score, it has some effect—usually five points or less.

3. *Paying off your credit will increase your score by 50 points.* Because of the complex (I mean really hard) algorithm of credit reporting, I can say this is simply untrue. There are hundreds of factors that go into determining our score. However, it's wise to pay your bills on time, work to lower your debts and make sure any inaccuracies are removed, or corrected.

4. *If I don't use credit cards, my score will be high.* Another myth to chalk up to inaccurate information. Not using credit cards means your credit score has a ratio of zero (saying you have no debt at all). This may actually hurt your score since it doesn't demonstrate that you can use your credit responsibly. Your credit utilization ratio is calculated for all of your cards, both individually and cumulatively. Having a high ratio on a single card could cause a red flag. The cumulative utilization carries a bit more weight.

5. *Your credit score and report are the same.* A credit report is just that, a detailed report of a person's credit history. There are three major credit bureaus, TransUnion, Equifax, and Experian. Each credit bureau will have their own report requirements.

A credit score is a three-digit number between 300 and 850. It tells a lender how risky you are and provides information regarding your credit usage, on-time payments, and the availability of credit. When you request your credit report, the credit score will be provided separately.

Have you ever heard these myths before? Did you believe them?

You Control Your Own Money Story

We all have a money story. It's the relationship that we form with our money over time. Your story can also be based on your circumstances. Some are wonderful, others are filled with pain, hurt, stress and even a little confusion. Most of our stories are a continuation of our parents because we tend to imitate what we see and hear. As you grow older, you start to combine what you have been taught by your parents plus your own experiences. This is how you begin to develop your own story.

Remember, your story can be whatever you wish as long as you are willing to do the work. Believe me, my story has changed several times during my life. I have a pretty awesome money story now, but it hasn't always been that way. As a child, my story was controlled by my mom because she earned and spent the money. We shared a just enough and sometimes a little more money story. As I described in chapter one-American standards said my mother and I were poor, but we had some excellent experiences with what we did have.

As I mentioned, my mom worked at least two jobs, sometimes three, to make ends meet when I was younger. I'm sure we had some savings and fun money because we were able to take vacations to see family and travel with our church. But when I became a teenager, I gained more control over my story. However, I began to make terrible financial decisions; which continued on through college and the early part of my twenties.

It wasn't until I was 25 years old and living back at home with my mom, because of my bad decisions, that I decided to shift my mindset to create a better money story.

Throughout the years I have been adding on to this story, some savvy financial decisions and some not so smart. Sometimes your financial downfalls can happen at any point in your life and at no fault of your own.

Life's experiences have a remarkable way of teaching lessons. It's up to you to be a student and learn from them. Take notes along your financial fitness journey and change the things you don't like while nurturing the stuff you do. Understand your why and use your S.M.A.R.T.E.R. goals as a foundation to help create the framework for your future accomplishments.

Chapter 10

Being Intentional

If you want to *ROCK Your Money*, you must learn to be intentional. It's one of the most powerful keys to living a financially fit life. It's sitting down and thinking about what you want out of life and how you plan to achieve it. There will always be something you want to splurge on, that one thing you must have. Maybe it's your most favorite thing to do, or that bucket list trip you always wanted to take.

You're going to run into conflicting priorities, unexpected expenses, impulse purchases, demands from your family—all of these things will put your money story to the test. When you meet these financial challenges, don't shy away from them—take control! I suggest you ask yourself a few questions, and please be honest with yourself. These questions and your answers will determine if you're on the right path to financial fitness.

Question #1 - Does this decision align with the goals you have set for yourself?

For example, let's say you're saving for a new home. Well, Christmastime rolls around, and you have children—of course you want them to have a very merry Christmas. You've already set aside your Christmas budget to purchase gifts for them. However, they have their own idea of what they want. You run off to the store to price the items and they are all over your budget. You love your kids, and you want to make them happy—but spending $200 on a new video game is not the best decision, right? Your long-term goals (like giving your family a new home for years to come) can sometimes be at odds with your short-term goals (like making your kids happy at the moment), and striking a balance between them is what being intentional is all about.

Question #2 - Is this decision worth my time or effort?

If your child is anything like my daughter, they're only going to play a game until the next best thing comes out (which is usually as quick as you can get it out of the box). There goes money that I could have saved towards purchasing my home. Think about it—you work pretty hard to earn your money. Often, we put our goals on the back burner to make someone else happy, pushing us off our target. Now, I'm not saying don't spend any money on your loved ones, but make sure you ask yourself the question: can you afford it?

Question #3 - *Can you afford to make this decision?*

Often, we spend money that we don't have by using credit cards we can't afford. Have you ever fooled yourself by saying, *I'll just buy this now and pay it off at the end of the month*? I've heard that one before. When the end of the month arrives, you think, *Well, I'll pay it off next month.* When your monthly statement arrives, your one-time payment has now accrued interest. Not just regular interest, either—this is your second month with a balance, so your interest has compounded. I hate it when that happens—and now you have a larger balance to pay.

This is why you need to ask yourself which spending decisions are really worth it to you. You know how hard you're working, and how hard you've *been* working for a long time. Those little impulse-buys at the moment can add up, and they can really undermine you. If you're not keeping your spending in line with your goals, you can end up being your own worst enemy—yes, even worse than the debt collectors who are always blowing up your phone!

Think carefully about those three questions—if the answer is "no" to any of them, you really should rethink your spending decisions. You must be fully aware of your money story and manage it so that you feel secure, have peace of mind, and quality of life that you and your family will enjoy.

My intention in writing this book is to give you a clear plan of action that can be followed as-is or tweaked to fit your ideas and goals.

Know Your Worth

"Know your numbers, you never know
when it will come in handy."

~Coach Fe~

Chapter 11

Calculating Your Net Worth

If I were to ask you what your net worth is would you know? Let me ask a better question, do you know what it means? Don't feel bad if you don't, you're not alone. Most people don't know what it means nor do they know their net worth.

Simply put, your net worth is the overall value of your goods and possessions less what you owe. In other words, it's the total value of your assets less liabilities. Follow the example on the following page and let's calculate your net worth:

Add Assets:

Savings Account- $10,000

Retirement Account-	$50,000
Home Value-	$200,000
Checking Account-	$3,000

Subtract Liabilities

Credit Cards-	($7,000)
Student Loans-	($15,000)
Other Debt-	($4,000)
Mortgage-	($105,000)
Net Worth =	***$132,000***

You may have other items that I have not included above, such as stock, pension, car notes, etc. Your ultimate goal is to have a positive net worth. The higher your number, the better your net worth. If your number is negative, don't fret it just means you need to work a little more on decreasing your debt, earning more money and increasing your possessions. Negative Net worth does not always mean your financial health is not good. It can mean that for right now you have more liabilities than assets. As time goes on you may start to see this number shift to the positive side a little more.

Calculating your net worth can help identify where you are spending too much money. Do you recall in Chapter 7, we talked about wants vs. needs? This is where that exercise comes in handy. Review your expenses and figure out what items you can do without. Your needs should represent 70% of your debt.

- 50% should include rent/mortgage, bills, loan payments, food, and other necessities.
- 20% should consist of your financial goals such as savings and investments.

Two of your goals should be to get rid of unnecessary spending before it starts and to reduce your current debt. It can be hard for women to evaluate their net worth really. It means you have to assess all your wants and needs. Sometimes the one thing that makes us feel good about ourselves is the one thing we can't afford. Objects or things should never define who you are- there is a vast difference between net worth and self–worth.

Net-Worth Does Not Equal Self-Worth

I believe in money management and building a financially fit life. However, I don't believe in valuing money so much you lose yourself in the process. Why women connect their self-worth to their net worth, I'm not quite sure. But it is hazardous to attach having money and things to how you feel about yourself. What happens if you fall on hard times? Your self-worth does not decrease because you don't have a lot of money. Self-worth should never be directly related to how much money you have. Life is not just about money or things, but I didn't always live by my own philosophy and beliefs.

I am reminded of a quote I learned years ago by an unknown author, "Money is a good servant but a bad master." Meaning, money is a useful tool, but it's not meant to run your life. We all have different things that motivate us, that make us feel like we have arrived. It may be a top of the line automobile or that big house in the ritzy part of town.

For me it's handbags, I *love* wearing my money- not really but that's what I think of when I buy an expensive hand bag. Think about it. I remember taking my mom and daughter on a weekend trip to Charleston, SC. I was going to get that special handbag. The one that people stopped and paid attention to, the one that made me feel like my status had changed slightly.

I was very excited when I walked through the doors. The service was different from other stores. The retail associates were as happy to see me as I was to be there (of course they're so glad I'm about to spend a grand on a bag). "How may I help you?" The sales lady asked. "I would like to see the Louis Vuitton Graceful handbag," I responded. I had the biggest kool-aide smile on my face when she sat the bag in my hands. It was perfect!

I tried it on to see if I liked the feel of it on my arm. Who was I fooling? I already knew I was going to buy the bag. I had been looking at it for months, and it was all mine now.

The packaging, the service, the store - my whole experience was beautiful. I walked out of that store feeling better about myself because I had "my thing". You know, that thing that proved I was relevant. Guess what? A couple of months later my precious Louis Vuitton purse, that I had to have, was just a thing. I still had the same issues.

Having that pretty, expensive bag on my arm really had not changed anything. I hate to say it, but I also felt a little regret. Ultimately, I realized my self-worth was not attached to the purse. It just made me feel good for a little while.

Self-worth is found within and is not attached to things. How many people do you know that make a lot of money, but are still broke, filing bankruptcy and living check to check? These people most likely attached their value to their salary. They probably haven't discovered what money is really for. I have said it several times, "Money is a Tool."

Women often tie their self-worth to how many times they have failed in life. I say don't be afraid to fail. This is when you learn and build character. Think about when you first learned how to ride a bike. How many times did you fall? How many times did you get up and get back on that bike? As a child, you were not afraid because you were on a mission, you had a why. You wanted to ride your bike and have fun doing it. That same mindset applies here. The one thing that has changed is you're an adult, and your bike has turned into another challenge. A bigger, better, sometimes scarier one. This may sound weird, but I tell my clients if you fail quickly and fail often, you will find your sweet spot.

Building self-worth is much like setting the foundation of your home. Your foundation holds firm even when it rains hard and the soil around it is wet. When the wind blows hard, or if you live in my area where hurricanes hit, the house may have experienced damage, but the foundation remains intact. Like that foundation, your self-worth will also stay intact if it is grounded in the right way. Always remember your '*Why*', focus on your goals.

Chapter 12

Creating Your Sweet Spot

Have you ever had a day where all the stars were aligned and everything was going your way? A day where every decision you made was a good one and resulted in a win-win situation. If you have, welcome to what I call The Sweet Spot.

When you're in the sweet spot everything is aligned and starts working for your benefit. At this point you start to see some of your dreams coming to life. You have: *Realized Your Money Potential, Owned Your Financial Destiny, Created Your Own Money Story, and you Know Your Worth-* you're in the sweet spot. This is when you start really living in your destiny!

Today is the first blank page in the rest of your life story. Are you ready to fill those pages with lasting memories? If you want to travel, book it! If wealth is what you want, it's yours to have. You simply must do the work to achieve your desired outcome. Use this book as a guide and adjust the steps to fit your lifestyle.

Make a commitment to yourself and your goals and always be true to who you are. Everyone's idea of their best life is not the same. Your plan may be having a beautiful house and being able to provide for your family. While someone else may want to travel to exotic places, and that's okay. Your best life is based on your own personal definition of what makes you happy, not those around you. This could also change as you go through different phases of your life.

Your best life belongs to you. It is yours to enjoy, but there are a couple of things you need to do first. If you want to reap the rewards that are coming to you, you have to organize your life and your finances. Stop making emotional decisions when it comes to your money.

I understand if you are experiencing an emergency, but remember, you are supposed to have an emergency fund set up for that. It feels horrible to miss an opportunity that you have been waiting for because you made a bad financial decision.

Don't go blindly into the future, think about it now. Set goals that support your ultimate dreams no matter how big they are. If you don't believe anything else I have told you, believe this: if you plan it, you are more likely to achieve it. If you don't already know how to achieve your goals, ask for help from a professional like myself. Someone that can offer you advice when you need it.

Try to avoid naysayers. You know who they are, the people that always tell you what you can't do. Most of the time it is because their small minds can't comprehend anything that is beyond their normal life.

Everything may not happen in your timeframe, but if you exercise a little patience (I call it stick and stay) you will reach your sweet spot. Most importantly don't give up on your dreams because things aren't going as planned. As Americans, we want everything now; however, the quick and easy way is not always the best way.

If you truly want to *R.O.C.K Your Money* take the time to do the work. Read this book over and over again if needed and ask for help if you find yourself in a financial situation you can't handle. At the end of the day it's your money, your life and your future to do whatever you want.

To jumpstart your journey, I have put together 25 of my most powerful tips. Each one builds upon the next to create the framework needed to shift your mind set and money to achieve financial success and create a financially fit life.

Get ready to ROCK Your Money!

~ 25 Powerful Money Tips ~

1. Start teaching your children how to manage their finances *before* they start their first job. Yes, that means beginning when they are a teenager excited about having their own money.

2. Change your mindset, change your life. It's as simple as that.

3. To achieve wealth, you must first see it. Visualizing your goals gives you something to work towards.

4. Understand the *why* behind your financial fitness journey. Find your motivation.

5. Financial fitness is 80% behavior and 20% knowledge.

6. Create SMARTER goals and kick butt achieving them.

7. Create a spending plan (budget) that tells your money where to go instead of wondering where it went. A spending plan will help decrease impulsive spending.

8. Your spending allowance is what is left after saving, investing and paying your expenses. Practice paying yourself first.

9. There is no benefit to carrying a balance on your credit card. Paying your bill monthly will ensure interest does not accrue on your account.

10. Don't close your credit cards. Closing credit cards will decrease your credit utilization rate along with your credit limit which will increase your credit to debt ratio.

11. Know how much you owe. It's important to track your spending.

12. Increase your income by changing your job or finding money you already have.

13. Read some type of financial media at least once a week to stay informed of what is going on in the world.

14. Don't try to keep up with the Joneses'.

15. Don't get upset if you have a financial setback, get up and keep moving forward.

16. Financial change happens when you are tired of doing the same old thing and expecting a different outcome.

17. Understand your debt doesn't disappear because you ignore it.

18. Start saving for later while you're young this will help you achieve your dreams in the future.

19. Be responsible if you decide to use credit.

20. Budgeting is smart and impulsive spending is senseless.

21. Live less out of habit and more out of intention.

22. Life is a series of choices that you must navigate.

23. Know your numbers.

24. Stay focused on your goals.

25. Enjoy "The Sweet Spot".

About the Author

Felicia V. Petit-Frere, affectionately known as Coach Fe, is a savvy financial coach. With 22 years of experience in the finance industry, Felicia provides premium coaching services to individuals who struggle with maintaining, managing, and balancing their finances. She is the CEO of Windsong Financial Coaching LLC. In her business, she teaches her clients how to become financially fit. She believes that everyone makes unfortunate financial decisions, but with the right help they can change their mindset and become more focused on being financially successful.

As Felicia was researching content for *R.O.C.K. Your Money,* she realized that it's not just a book she has written; she wants to start a movement. A financial fitness movement that provides education and proven methods for those who are willing and ready to learn.

If you would like to learn more about Coach Fe or receive notifications when she is having an event, going live, or posting tips, you may contact her by email, website or social media:

Email: Felicia@WindsongFC.com
Website: www.WindsongFC.com

Facebook: www.facebook.com/coachfe1
Instagram: @_coachfe_
LinkedIn: www.linkedin.com/in/coachfe1/

Remember, you must tell your money where to go or you will wonder where it went. ~ Coach Fe~

Realize Your Money Potential

Own Your Financial Destiny

Create Your Own Money Story

Know Your Worth

You only get one beautiful life to live and one chance to live it. Dream big and make this life the best one ever. Take the time to create your plan and kick butt achieving it.

"R.O.C.K. Your Money"

~Coach Fe

www.ingramcontent.com/pod-product-compliance
Lightning Source LLC
Chambersburg PA
CBHW021421210526
45463CB00001B/478